"Oy! Only six? Why not more?"

SIX-WORD MEMOIRS ON JEWISH LIFE

D0880667

from **SMITH Magazine** and **Reboot**

Edited by **Larry Smith**

For information on ordering books at a reduced rate for your school,

synogogue, book club or organization, see **www.smithmag.net/books**.

SECOND EDITION

Designer: Gail Ghezzi

Cover by Nicole Salzano

Library of Congress Cataloging-in-Publication Data is available upon request.

ISBN 978-0-9847350-1-3

Everyone has a story. What's yours?

www.smithmag.net

Introduction

I f you had exactly six words to describe your life, what would they be? That's the challenge we posed to readers of SMITH Magazine, the online storytelling community I founded in 2006. We called these short life stories "Six-Word Memoirs," a reinvention of the form that, according to literary lore, Hemingway birthed when he was challenged to write a whole novel in just six words ("For sale: baby shoes, never worn.") in a bar bet.

Our Six-Word Memoir® project has since taken on a life beyond our wildest expectations. More than six years and half a million stories later on **SMITHmag.net** and **SMITHteens.com**, it has become a bestselling book series and board game, a teaching tool used across the world and a powerful way to spur on self-expression for anyone and everyone. Preachers and rabbis alike have embraced six-word prayers as a way to distill faith. In hospitals and veterans' groups, after-school programs and speed dating services, Six-Word Memoirs have been used to foster understanding, ease communication and break the ice.

The six-word limitation forces us to figure out the essence of who we are and what matters most. This simple form of expression can become the starting point for larger discussions. And that's exactly what we hope will happen with the latest chapter in the six-word story, *Six-Word Memoirs on Jewish Life*. This book contains 360 Six-Word Memoirs that offer personal windows into the wild, weird and wonderfully complex world of Judaism today. We hope this book starts many conversations about the meaning of Jewish life among Jews and non-Jews alike, in synagogues and churches, among both the most Orthodox and most secular.

"Many hands have kept me afloat," offers the writer Nick Flynn (not a Jew) in our first book, *Not Quite What I Was Planning: Six-Word Memoirs by Writers Famous & Obscure*. Nick's words are the perfect six-word sentiment for a project that is the work of so many people. First and foremost, I want to thank my partner in this project, Reboot, a nonprofit organization whose mission is to start discussions about Jewish identity, community and meaning—precisely the purpose of this book. Reboot's Roger Bennett, Amelia Klein and Dina Mann offered sage wisdom. Reboot has brought so many wonderful people into my life, including Amy Rothberger, who served as a valuable editor on this book and created the glossary found in the back. If there's a word or expression you don't know it's most likely explained there.

SMITH associate editor Meredith Sires, along with interns Yael Roberts and Elizabeth Crowder, were indispensible members of a small, terrific team. Thanks also to Randy Lutterman and the JCAA, Harlene Winnick Appelman and the Covanent Foundation, Carolyn Hessel and the Jewish Book Council, Benjamin Maron and InterFaithFamily.com, Morlie Levin and Birthright Israel NEXT, Jeff Newelt and *Heeb*, Aaron Bisman, Rebecca Guber, Gary Belsky and Karen Golden.

When you watch the video at sixwordmemoirs.com/jewish that accompanies this book and wonder, *Where do they get that incredible soundtrack?*, you'll know why I'm so grateful for David Katznelson and the Idelsohn Society for Musical Preservation. And the book's title? It's the gift of prolific sixer Elisa Shevitz, who, upon hearing of this project, exclaimed, "Oy! Only six? Why not more?"

With each story on SMITH Magazine our community becomes stronger and more interesting. I hope you'll share your story about Jewish life or any part of your life at sixwordmemoirs.com

Larry Smith
Founder, SMITH Magazine

"My Jewish genealogy ironically reveals 'blacksmiths'."

SIX-WORD MEMOIRS ON JEWISH LIFE

We are not a concise people.

– *Joel Stein*

**Newly Jewish
but an old soul.**

– *Erin Hoagland*

Circumcision
has been least
challenging part.

– *Dan Rollman*

613 rules, one soul set free.

– *Russ Roberts*

Blonde shiksa births Jewish daughter, self.

– Amanda Keckonen Clayman

I worry if I don't worry.

– Leena Prasad

Chicken is central to the story.

– Annie Lumerman

Everything with us a question, why?

– Mark Rosenblum

In cahoots: Optometrists
and Talmud publishers.

– Rabbi Toby Manewith

Had Bar Mitzvah.
Still not man.

– Aaron Kisslinger

Everything great
came from summer camp.

– Craig Kanarick

God chose. Said no.
Now what?

– Adam Blackman

Don't count, sat in services anyway.

– Kellen Kaiser

**Jewish
star
atop our
Christmas tree.**

– A.J. Jacobs

Excessive rumination from
eating only ruminants.

– Jonathan Freund

Wait, you've got a
little schmutz.

– Michele Reznik

Half Jewish.
Half Italian.
Totally stuffed.

– Dave Cirilli

A pronounced weakness for smoked fish.

– Adam Levy

Mourning missing out on Jewish childhood.

– Ally Reece

Wasn't expecting to miss Hebrew school.

– Audrey Lang

Family spends meals discussing other meals.

– Jana Loeb

**Hypocrite:
Prays to God,
uses JDate.**

– *Aimee Randall*

**Never too late
to become Muslim...**

– *Adi Talby*

You're gay? L'chaim!
He's goyishe? Shonda!

– *Adam Pollack*

The best hair, the worst spilkes.

– *Joanna Arkans*

From Trochenbrod,
a renewed story unfolds.
— *Esther Safran Foer*

I do not stand idly by.
— *Daniel Schwartz*

Eight Chanukah nights.
Feels like thirty.

– Ayelet Waldman

Sunday night?
Yes, lobster is kosher.

– Floyd Skloot

"Avinu Malkeinu,"
my favorite melancholy song.

– Angelina Love

My grandmother's tattoo dominates my nightmares.

– Lux Alptraum

No sacrament. Just brisket. Take charge.

– Rachel Gross-Prinz

Jew in Arkansas?
Vey iz mir.

– Amos Lassen

From talit to tichel.
Always evolving.

– Melissa Scholten-Gutierrez

Prayer begins with questions
not answers.

– Alanna Sklover

Nazi's daughter saved
by Jewish Manhattan.

– Anna Steegmann

Rabbi's sermons are
lullabies
with meaning.

– Max Sterenson

Found my people, if not God.

–Christopher Noxon

I kvetch.
And therefore, I am.

– Elizabeth Kalman

Loved the food,
hated the shiva.

– David Hirshey

The Torah's story tells me mine.

– Devorah Spilman

One Jewish book changed the world.

– Carolyn Hessel

More Phillip Roth than David Lee.

– Charles London

Every meal is a *Seinfeld* episode.

– Karen Golden

Started off kosher. Then, discovered bacon.

– Anna Wexler

Born with big nose.
Pursued comedy.

– Andy Borowitz

Half Jewish, half Armenian: All survivor.

– Amy Keyishian

Visited Dead Sea,
returned with Life.

– John Wilder

Definitely still wandering,
but
not
lost.

– Ruthie Garelik

Comedic fire:
rub two schticks together.

– Ed Small

My Judaism is somatic: blood, bone.

– Ellen Rosen

A quarter Jewish. Do I count?

– Heather Dearly

Best part of Judaism:
         menschy men.

– Amy Friedman

Married Christian.
Gaydar works, Jewdar broken.

– Michael Forster Rothbart

**The Manischewitz
made me do it.**

– Maya Stein

I'm the Messiah..

so are You.

– Amichai Lau-Lavie

My grandparents got out.
I'm here.

– Erika Dreifus

Chopping liver, telling jokes.
Too schmaltzy?

– Dan Fost

Suspended disbelief for the Bar Mitzvah.

– Neil Fine

Mom: "Jewish boys don't play football."

– Michael Areinoff

Sick of sharing
birthday with Jesus.

– Cathy Alter

Big Jewish fish.
Small gentile pond.

– David Baum

Live,
lose,
learn,
love,
laugh: L'chaim!

– *Susan Barnes*

Family tree:
      lots of zaftig women.

– *Vicky Botnick*

Children breathing in my Jewish heart.

– *Mark Horowitz*

Goy says "Oy!"
after meeting family.

– *Drew Brockington*

Gay Jew puts
Judy in Judaism.

– *Michael Getty*

"**Finish eating...people starving in Europe.**"

– *Stephanie Andelman*

Tikkun Olam.
Gemilut Chasadim.
Mel Brooks.

– *Ian Zaback*

Prostate hurts from all the grief.

– *Gary Shteyngart*

Ate too much,
prayed too little.

– Jennifer Small

Traditions to transmit: God, not guilt.

– Matthue Roth

Impressive Hasidic lineage. Dating a Catholic.

– Aliza Bartfield

Overstuffing is part
of my aesthetic.

– Bill Bragin

Jew by choice
finds her voice.

– Gwen Wexler

I like Palestinians. Get over it.

– Sara Gunning

**The Torah's God:
a bipolar adolescent.**

– Michael Castleman

Paying retail is against
my religion.

– Jennifer Baron

No way to escape the mishegas.

– Jackie Leventhal

Oh, right.
This too shall pass.

– Adene Sacks

Jesus may save, but Moses invests.

– *Mel Alper*

Sorry, I can't stop feeding you.

– *Naomi Adiv*

Taught children;
now they teach me.

– *Ron Burton*

**Mani. Schvitz. Manischewitz.
Rinse, lather, repeat.**

– *Emily Hirshey*

Tunisian Sephardi rejected for NAACP scholarships.

– *Erik Levis*

Living Torah means always
having gratitude.

– *Jeremy Rovinsky*

Vermont Jew:
sukkah in a parka.

– *Renee Woliver*

From this you make a living?

– *Sophie Rosenblum*

I should have
had the chicken.

– Larry David

"Putz! Schmuck! Noodnik! Nebbish!"
"Sheket, Dad!"

– *Jim Gladstone*

Have faith in asking many questions.

– *Rachel Kramer Bussel*

Former monochromatic wardrobe
now seeking color.

– *Yaakov Hellinger*

Smash that glass,
tap that ass.

– *Sheri Knauth*

Adam Sandler, update your Chanukah list.

– Laura Horwitz

"Your voice sounds thinner **today, darling."**

– Abby Ellin

Preserve the past.
Be the future.

– Shauna Waltman

Yid dish is a kosher meal.

– Al Jaffee

When life meets Torah,
blessings emerge.
                    – Jen Gubitz

Constantly balancing
between
visits, guilt trips.
                    – Meredith Sires

Shiksa wife more Jewish than me.
                    – Andy Goodman

Covenant: blessing and burden. My choice.
                    – Natalie Pullen

It's different. And I like that.

– Nicole Goldstein

To Florida! Annual migration with birds.

– Jim Berman

Lapsed, cultural, and now professional Jew.

– Michael Kaminer

Leviticus: Love your neighbor as yourself.

– Rabbi Seth Adelson

Be a mensch; pass it on.

– Marsha Stein

I can't;
I have a blister.

– Daniel Okrent

Shabbat:
Eight Jews,
twelve dietary restrictions.

– Jamie Levine Daniel

Learned my Judaism
at pro-choice rally.

– Rabbi Sari Laufer

Free will:
God plans, man laughs.

– *Yael Roberts*

Plowing our texts for pertinent meaning.

– *Christopher Orev Reiger*

Latkethon at my mother's
gynecologist's home.

– *Erica Fishbein*

Jews in
groups make
me nervous.

– *Gary Belsky*

Protocols, shmotocols. Just gimme the Zion.

– Gideon Lichfield

One RV mezuzah.
Two wandering Jews.

– Amy Beth Oppenheimer

Bat Mitzvah. Menstruation.
Same day?
Womanhood!

– Amanda Chudnow

Thought Yiddish.
Married British.
Oy! Oi!

– Rachel Pine

Baruch Ata Adonai Elohainu... um... uh...

– Mary McConnell

Like Zusya,
trying to be me.

– Rabbi Steven Rubenstein

At 55, considering a Bat Mitzvah.

– Cheryl Corson

Is he Jewish?
Is he Jewish?

– Shoshana Berger

What's most Jewish is my atheism.

– Molly Crabapple

Lubavitch Chabadnik asks: "Jewish?"
Me: "No."

– Douglas Rushkoff

God, are you with me now?

– Nicola Behrman

My identity but not my politics.

– Naomi Levy

Born Orthodox Jew.
Now Orthodox cynic.

– Molly Bee

Never fulfilled Bat Mitzvah speech expectations.

– Robin Beth Schaer

Trans, Jewish. Don't need a mohel.

– Mel King

**One subject,
endless opinions,
all talk.**

– Lesley Stein

Jewish vegetarian:
Only miss gefilte fish.

– Hilary Bothma

**Thought God punished.
I was wrong.**

– Josh Radnor

Repairing world:
until Messiah, our job.

– Elaine Lavine

Why worry?
History suggests it's advisable.

– Dinah Finkelstein

God giveth.
God taketh away.
Goddamnit.

– Jacob Berkman

Davening. An introduction to early sciatica.

– *Rich Shadrin*

Hid comics inside Hebrew school textbooks.

– *Jeff Newelt*

I wonder about God. Truth? Fiction?

– *Ben Greenman*

Webcast Yom Kippur services. Strangely satisfying.

– *Amy Ramos*

Guilty overachiever
seeking spirituality
and
patience.

– Judith Rose

Torah wellsprings
water my parched soul.

– Blumi Mishulovin

Living the truth that all's *echad*.

– Marni Rothman

Woody Allen is my personal lullaby.

– Jeni Janson

Used up my six words
complaining.

– Michelle Wolfson

Endless vista,
always present,
usually hidden.

– David Glickman

Choice through knowledge —
your steps alone.

– Aimee Weiss

World
is
narrow
bridge,
be
brave!

– Marci Bellows

No, not related.
Horowitz: Judaism's "Smith."

– Adam Horowitz

"House of bondage" jokes, funny annually.

– Rachel Sklar

**I'll bet Jesus
found the afikomen.**

– Steven Wolfe

Mom and God had boundary issues.

– Marty Kaplan

You never write,

you never call.

– Susan Silver

Tikkun Olam
  is my raison d'être.

– *Melissa Reitkopp*

**Build a better world.
No excuses.**

– *Matt Fieldman*

Six years old; puked on Masada.

– Rachel Shukert

Breast milk is pareve.
Weird kashrut.

– Abigail Greenbaum

This is a Roman nose, OK?

– Jason Biggs

Eat, Love, Pray;
Eat, Love;
Eat.

– Fred Scherlinder Dobb

**See, Mom,
I'm a doctor. (Ph.D.)**

– Jerry Heyman

At least you know he's circumcised.

– Amy Schumer

I'm a Jew. Joke, I do.

– Abby Kuhns

Crosses don't work
on Jewish vampires.

– Satya Tretiak

Skiing?
A person could get hurt.

– *Arnold Simon*

**Judaism: Tradition, innovation
messily rolled together.**

– *Sara Steinman*

God is in
the
small details.

– *Shanni Profesorsky*

Less oy. More joy. Learn. Celebrate.

– *Deborah Lipstadt*

I use chutzpah
as an aphrodisiac.

– *Amy Rothberger*

Deli food always
beats
fine dining.

– *Rozzie Heeger*

Chicken soup!
With or without kreplach?

– *Dr. Alan M. Reznik*

Pastrami is the spice of life.

– *Avi Flamholz*

**Love the food,
hate the sanctimony.**

– *Norman Wilner*

Putting *some* pep in my *schlep*.

– Ashley Allen

Rogachev, Harbin, Havana,
Sydney, Philadelphia,
Next?

– Amelia Klein

I was in need.
Heard: Hineini.

– Elissa Froman

Traditional sederists.
Culinary matzachists. Passover *chazers*.

– Samuel Basch

Chicken fat
makes life worth living.

– Jane and Michael Stern

Wait, is your kippah actually edible?

– Aaron Laurito

An intense love affair with God!

– *JoAnne Shapiro*

They got paté. We got ptcha.

– *Mark Lamster*

Presbyterian school rebel, Hollywood shabbos-keeper.

– *Rob Kutner*

Saying Kaddish. Missing you. Remembering. Remembering.

– *Debra Darvick*

I discovered myself through being Jewish.

– Sarah Ducker

Youth group, camp, Israel, rabbinate, family.

– Greg Kanter

Nobody told my hormones I'm Orthodox.

– Eliana Block

Mother, our lady of perpetual dissatisfaction.

– Jennifer Glick

Shakespeare Shmakespeare;
we've got Philip Roth!

– *Raymond Simonson*

**Threat of extinction breeds
Jewish excellence.**

– *Tovah Feldshuh*

My grandma
would be so proud.

– *Greg Clayman*

Judaism accesses
fuller humanity positive,
negative.

– *Beth Kissileff*

Million,
million,
million,
million,
million,
million?

– Hadassah Gross

Judaism:
5,000 years of terrible candy.

– Gail Lerner

You were right Mom, it matters.

– Mitzi Druss

Strong opinion, biting humor,
warm heart.

– Lori Warren

Christmas:
Thank God for Chinese restaurants.

– Tamara Straus

Only keep kosher in the diaspora.

– *Mara Berman*

I need more
Bar Mitzvah money.

– *Jack Grubman*

Hindu Jew seeks light
in everything.

– *Marc Mannheimer*

Real bagels don't
have jalapeño peppers.

– *Paul Beckman*

Jewish summer camp, my *etz chayim*.

– *Ari J. Shapiro*

**Texas Bar Mitzvah.
Bacon-wrapped shrimp.**

– *Jeremy Goldberg*

Neurotic Jew
neurotic about her neuroses.

– *Danielle Sherman*

Half Jewish.
Sadly, not Lenny Kravitz.

– *Max Bachhuber*

Gedolei Yisrael: Fonzie, Hyman, Kaminsky, Konigsberg.

– Tony Michels

German-Jews. Dyslexia. Acting. Family. Writing. Complete.

– Henry Winkler

**Raised Arkansas Baptist.
Now Detroit Jew.**

– Gayla Bassham

Thought "klutz" was term
of endearment.

– Jacqueline Rice

**Family disappointment?
My hatred of lox.**

– Robin Gelfenbien

Six words,
six hundred thirteen opinions.

– Bryan Kort

Neurotic hypochondriac
seeks medical attention,
please.

– *Jessica Lester*

Not exactly Chosen. More like inducted.

– *Coleen Goodson*

Genesis, Exodus, Leviticus,
Numbers, ummmm, Duderroneous.

– *Rabbi Stephen Landau*

Hair: liability turned asset; still thick.

– *Ben Falik*

Gluten-free life is Passover year round.

– Naomi Jill Wolf

Old parchment scrolls
soothe weary souls.

– Michael J. Sullivan

Apocalypse is when
pickles run out.

– Paul Ratner

Question everything.
Eat everything. Feel bad.

– Jenji Kohan

I thought I caught a gefilte!

– Ryan Eastman

I've learned I'm really
more Jew-*ish*.

– Dana Kader Robb

Others have history;
we have memory.

– Alexandra Benjamin

Did you call your mother today?

– Lisa Soble Siegmann

We bonded over our deviated septums.

– *Alessandra Rizzotti*

Black gay ex-Christian woman now Jewish.

– *Erika Davis*

Dim sum is our Sunday school.

– *Liza Wyles*

Shoah shadows.
Vibrant life.
Hopeful future.

– *Rachel Dubelu*

Favorite Jewish ballplayers:
Greenberg, Koufax and...

– Louis Smith

Wondering: Madonna helping or hurting us?

– The Sklar Brothers

**Carbohydrates
call my name every day.**

– Mary Petersdorf

Love people always.
Rest is commentary.

– Joelle Novey

613 rules, who has the koach?

– Hadass Segal

Do good.
Be kind.
Thank God.

– Anita Diamant

**Lightbulb needs changing.
Call a handyman.**

– Amy Feldman

**Uncle Saul's commandment:
"Meals need seltzer!"**

– Gail Ghezzi

Sh'ma Yisrael Adonai
Eloheinu Adonai Echad.

– Deuteronomy

The Sh'ma,
my favorite six words.

– Xander Karsten

Bar Mitzvah video

used as blackmail.

— *Jon Papernick*

Chosen for something.
Not sure what...

– *Adam Clyne*

Yes,
I'm wearing a sweater,
Mom.

– *Mikey Franklin*

Romantic Jewess wishes
Chanukah featured mistletoe.

– *Elisa Shevitz*

"But you just don't look Jewish."

– *Elizabeth Wurtzel*

Not shomer Shabbat.
Too much homework.

– Sarah Rubock

Israel means "to wrestle."
Explains everything.

– Tiffany Shlain

I am always filled with angst.

– Juliet Simmons

The hora is the best part.

– Gillian Zoe Segal

Coolest kid at Yeshiva. Still nerdy.

– Jason Klein

We embrace tradition
but reject convention.

– Edward Harwitz

**My Tikkun Olam
includes your enemies.**

– Sharon McKellar

Bring a date to my ∫hiva.

– Steven Liss

Thanks for the blue eyes, Cossacks.

– Lisa Brown

Read right
to left
for him.

– Lindsey Digangi

Secret law:
Maine Jews allowed lobster.

– Joel Rubin

Obligation and responsibility:
ennobling Jewish concepts.

– Ruth Messinger

Haggled.
Mistaken for Jewish.
Tremendously flattered.

– Laureatte Loy

Cooking chicken soup stirs
mother memories.

– Carol Smith

School bully throwing Bac-Os at Jews.

– Leonard White

Black Jew,
both outsiders
even here.

– Walter Mosley

Read Marx, Freud,
Talmud; still reading.

– *Anne Schiff*

Haggadah:
most radical book there is.

– *Jonathan Safran Foer*

I fantasize about
Avigdor from Yentl.

– *Jessica Berlin*

Enough tsuris to fill six books.

– *Rose Waldman*

Kissed a lady. Said shehecheyanu later.

– Elissa Vinnik

Choosing to be chosen,
best choice.

– Sarah Belknap

I'd prefer more
gelt than guilt.

– Patricia Carragon

**Got my nose done.
(Still circumcised.)**

– Michael Malice

Rabbi accidentally spoke of
"Shitting siva."

– Jo-Ellen Balogh

Post-denominational Jews eat Thai for Christmas.

– Shari Salzhauer Berkowitz

Zayde refuses to die
without great-grandchildren.

– Leslie Stonebraker

**Lost Judaism; found again.
I'm home.**

– Deborah Adler

Will eat bacon but refuses ham.

– Max Baumgarten

A life uncriticized is not Jewish.

– Lisa Wurtele

What page are we on again?

– Matthew Sheren

Got allowance.
Saved, spent,
gave tzedakah.

– Lisa Exler

Tattooed Jew seeks
entrance to Heaven.

– Elijah Aroha

Didn't know, started learning, still questioning.

– Debra Nussbaum Cohen

Remember where you're from.
And going.

– *Artie Gold*

Reason Jews joke:
life not funny.

– *Howard Jacobson*

**Thought Easter
was a zombie story.**

– Daniel Handler

Oh no, Oh no, Oh no.

– Maira Kalman

Wanna be righteous,
instead just anxious.

– *Jill Soloway*

Read, struggle,
discuss, resolve,
rinse, repeat.

– *Jason Menayan*

Converted to Judaism for the jokes.

– *Lorenzo Mattozzi*

Walter: "I don't roll on Shabbos!"

– *The Big Lebowski*

Yiddish makes even pleasantries sound filthy.

– *Karen Sulkis*

For sale. Pair tefillin. Never worn.

– *Roger Bennett*

Never accept gift horses.
Not kosher.

– *Paul Harrington*

I glory in my Jewish traditions.

– *Mayor Ed Koch*

Secret latke ingredient is knuckle blood.

– Rachel Fershleiser

**Shehecheyanu over garden tomato.
I'm Jewish.**

– Lisa Colton

Jewish model,
not a model Jew.

– Joshua Feldman

Oy.
So much room
for interpretation.

– Betsy Polk Joseph

Legacy of strong women in family.

– Joanne Brockington

Seeing God's face in your face.

– Rabbi Laura Geller

Don't know which Self to synopsize.

– Art Spiegelman

I have a fetish for altakockers.

— Amy Sohn

Half-Jewish: circumcised,
but circumspect about it.

— George Held

Today's puny teens,
tomorrow's Jewish leaders.

— Karen Katzoff

The guilt threats
mobilize family gatherings.

— Rebecca Guber

Observant means paying
very careful attention.

– *Sharon Price*

I wrestle with God.
Every day.

– *Cori Mancuso*

Perpetually longing for place in community.

– *Dara Wilensky*

Can't talk;
my hand is broken.

– *Ellen Ullman*

Displaced dad makes smoked meat sandwich.

– Hal Niedzviecki

Guilty admission: didn't hate Hebrew school.

– Jackie Miller

Books change lives.
They've changed mine.

– Joseph Telushkin

Who couldn't use a little Shabbat?

– Terri Ginsberg Bernsohn

**Grew up in Texas.
Shalom y'all.**

– Dayna Shaw

The Mamaloshen is in my heart.

– Dina Mann

**Reason not dogma,
joy not fear.**

– Amy Cohen

"Dad, six Jewish words?"
"Enough, Sandi!"

– Sandi DuBowski & Elliot DuBowski

Om Shalom:
Best of both worlds.

– Jeff Greenwald

Funky brown chick
throws Chanukah party.

– Twanna Hines

Faith is fine,
service fills souls.

– JJ Slatkin

Bacon brings me closer to God.

– Ray Richmond

Catching and releasing
"nice Jewish boys."

– Lisa Bottone

Prefer mechitza minyan
for the eye-candy.

– Ira Stup

Comic with guarenteed work
on Christmas.

– Ophira Eisenberg

Baruch atah Adonai, viva
Puerto-Rico ha'olam.

–Venessa Hidary

Born Mayflower descendent.
Avraham new ancestor.

– Marty Johnston

The comfort of so many questions.

– Linda Bernstein

Shalom.
That's such a great word.

– Josephine Collett

Proud Diasporans write
new history chapter.

– Jordana Horn

**They didn't kill us.
Let's eat!**

– Eileen Cukier

Ohio Orthodox equals
New York reform.

– Stan Friedman

Divine memoir:
Let there be light.

– Natalie Wood

Everybody knows one of your relatives.

– Joyce Gordon

Comedy, brains,
and belly to spare.

– Laurel Felt

G-d listens to a sound argument.

– Sandra Little

Nondairy creamer?
Effing kosher industrial complex.

– Dory Kornfeld

There's NO hole in the sheet!

– Jillian Scheer

I know, I know. The Holocaust.

– Judah Ariel

Table of ten,
        one bottle:
            dayenu.

– Robin Epstein

A smorgasbord of genetic diseases.
Hooray!

– David Wolkin

Treif dishes are for pepperoni
pizza.

– Lynn Goldberg

Not cool to scapegoat a Jew.

– *Terri Kay Emanuel*

Beautiful traditions I wish were mine.

– *Kimberly Shepherd*

**My first hangover:
post Bar Mitzvah.**

– *Mark Dommu*

Covenant matters.
Set example.
Judaism endures.

– *Monnie Newman*

Perpetually joining JDate.
Perpetually canceling JDate.

– Adri Cowan

I hope he finds neurotic erotic.

– Liz Nord

I guess I'd always been rabbi-curious.

– Lynn Harris

Not all Jewish boys are nice.

– *Michael Lucas*

Life is to dance Hava Nagila.

– *David Katznelson*

Connection with my people, not shul.

– *Deborah Sweet Kucinski*

Belong to something
bigger than me.

– *Amy Amiel*

Found Jewish princess.
Goodbye, succulent pork.

– Leah Damski

We read backward but think forward.

– Deborah Copaken Kogan

God said, "Do this."
Now what?

– Michael Kates

I was Jewish in another life.

– Don Letta

**No hell, really?
What a rip-off!**

– *Sascha Rothchild*

I'm going to worry about it.

–*Buck Henry*

No, Bubbe,
　　I'm not married yet.
–Gary Rozman

Looking for my b'shert.
You him?
–Robyn Faintich

Read *Portnoy's Complaint*, swore off liver.
– Lynn LeBlanc

In Hebrew, six words are ten.
–Janice Silverman Rebibo

Fourteen Rachels
in my address book.

– Larry Smith

"You don't wear a little hat?"

– Jaron Berliner

My people celebrate life every day.

– Elena Levitt

My number ends in 613.
Coincidence?

– Jeremy Tofler

I'm sick of talking about Jews.

–Shalom Auslander

Only writing this out of guilt.

– David Sax

Funny hats,
funny curls,
funny jokes.

– Dick Pasky

Still no clue. But tryin'.
L'chaim.

– Margie Howe

Zeks verter iz badir a mayse?
(By you six words is a story?)

– Eddy Portnoy

**Unsure of God?
You're cool here.**

– Emilia Diamant

Life finally converging
with absolute glee.

– Ali Adler

Birth bris bed bath and beyond.

– Barry Blitt

A wandering Jew
never says
goodbye.

– Richard Davis

A Glossary of Terms & Phrases

613 The number of mitzvot, or commandments, written in the Torah.

Afikomen The piece of matza hidden during the Passover seder. Usually children will search for it, and a prize is awarded to the child who finds it first.

Altakockers Yiddish term for old folks.

Avinu Malkeinu Literally: "Our Father, Our King." Refers to a well-known prayer of supplication said on and between Rosh Hashanah and Yom Kippur.

Baruch Ata Adonai Eloheinu The opening words of a Hebrew blessing. Translated as: "Blessed art thou, oh Lord our God."

B'shert One's destined mate or spouse; meant to be.

Bubbe Grandmother.

Chazers Literally: pigs. Idiomatically, people who are sloppy or greedy.

Davening Praying, often in a swaying or back-and-forth rocking motion.

Dayenu Refrain from a song in the Passover seder meaning "enough!"

Echad Hebrew word meaning "one."

Etz Chayim A Hebrew phrase that literally translates to "tree of life."

Gedolei Yisrael A Hebrew phrase meaning "the greats of Israel," used to describe the most revered thinkers or leaders of a generation, generally referring to rabbis.

Gefilte [Fish] Ashkenazi delicacy made of various kinds of ground fish. "Delicacy" tends to be a subjective term depending on one's palate.

Gemilut Chasadim Acts of righteousness. It is said that a good life is one of Torah, Mitzvot (commandments) and acts of righteousness.

Goy Yiddish word meaning "non-Jewish person," sometimes derogatory. Plural: goyim, adjective: goyish/goyishe.

Hineini Word meaning, "Here I am." It is said by Adam, Abraham and Moses in conversation with God to declare their presence, and is often used in modern-day Yom Kippur services and sermons.

Kaddish A prayer recited as part of the Jewish mourning rituals, following the passing of a loved one.

Kashrut/Kosher Jewish dietary laws. Often referred to as "keeping kosher."

Kippah Skull cap/head covering traditionally worn by men. Also called "yarmulke."

Koach Strength.

Kreplach Meat-filled dumpling often eaten in chicken soup.

Kvetch Yiddish word meaning to gripe or complain.

L'chaim Hebrew meaning "To life!" Used as exclamation in lieu of "cheers!"

Mamaloshen Yiddish term meaning "mother tongue" that refers to the Yiddish language.

Mechitza Partition in traditional synagogues used to separate the men's and women's sections.

Mensch Yiddish word for a good, upstanding person, usually a man.

Mezuzah Scroll hung on the doorposts of Jewish homes, containing the words of the *Sh'ma* (see below).

Minyan The ten-person minimum required to pray in a group service. Idiomatically refers to the service itself.

Mishegas Yiddish term meaning craziness. Idiomatically, also means business or fussiness.

Mohel Person who performs ritual circumcisions.

Pareve Term which implies a food has neither meat nor dairy designation.

Plotz Yiddish term meaning to collapse, faint or keel over in response to strong emotion (excitement, disappointment, surprise, exhaustion, etc.).

Ptcha Savory gelled dish made from bones (often calves feet), flavored with garlic and other spices.

Schmutz Yiddish word for filth or dirt.

Schvitz Literally: to sweat. A schvitz can also be a steam room or bath house.

Shabbat/Shabbos Sabbath day of rest.

Shehecheyanu Blessing said the first time one performs a given act.

Shiksa Yiddish term for non-Jewish woman, sometimes derogatory in its connotation.

Shiva The ritual seven-day mourning period where the bereaved are visited by friends, family and community members.

Schlep Yiddish word for to carry, haul, or trek in an inconvenient fashion.

Sh'ma Prayer translated as "Hear O Israel, the Lord our God, the Lord is One."

Schmaltzy Sentimental or sappy; overly kitschy. Derived from *schmaltz*, which literally translates to "rendered chicken fat."

Shoah Hebrew term for the Holocaust.

Shomer Shabbat The practice of keeping and observing the laws of the Sabbath.

Shonda An outrage, a shame, or a pity; a scandal.

Shul Yiddish term for synagogue.

Spilkes/Shpilkes Yiddish equivalent of "ants in your pants" — anxiety, jumpiness. Can stem from excitement or apprehension.

Sukkah An outdoor hut constructed to re-enact the temporary dwellings the Israelites lived in while wandering in the desert.

Talit A prayer shawl traditionally worn by men during morning services. In progressive streams of Judaism, sometimes also worn by women.

Tefillin Black leather box and straps worn (generally by men) during morning weekday prayers that contain scrolls with the text of the *Sh'ma.*

Tichel Head covering worn by religious women once they are married.

Tikkun Olam Concept of repairing the world through acts of community service, social justice, environmental action and other imperatives.

Treif Yiddish word for non-kosher.

Tsuris Yiddish word for problems or issues of worry/concern.

Tzedakah Literal meaning: righteousness or justice. Refers to charity.

Vey iz mir Yiddish term meaning "woe is me." Often follows "Oy" and is a term of exasperation.

Yarmulke Head covering traditionally worn by men. Also called "kippah."

Zaftig Having a full or shapely figure.

Zayde Grandfather.

Zusya Refers to Rabbi Zusya of Hanipol, the protagonist of a famous story which culminates in him saying, "When I die and go to the world to come, they will not ask me, 'Zusya, why were you not Moses?' They will ask me, 'Zusya, why were you not Zusya?'"

One life. Six words. What's yours?

Since the Six-Word Memoir® made its debut in 2006,
more than half a million short life stories have been shared
on the storytelling community SMITH Magazine. In classrooms
and boardrooms, churches and synagogues, veterans' groups
and across the dinner table, Six-Word Memoirs have
become a powerful tool to catalyze conversation,
spark imagination or simply break the ice.

Share a Six-Word Memoir or any part of your life at
www.sixwordmemoirs.com

Want This Book?

This book is published independently with the
support of the nonprofit, Reboot, and available
in select bookstores and online exclusively on
Blurb.com. Go to **www.bit.ly/onlysix**

Interested in a discounted large order? Contact
us at **news@smithmag.net** and let's talk!

About **SMITH Magazine**

Founded in January 2006 with the tagline,
"Everyone has a story. What's yours?" SMITH Magazine has
become a leader in personal storytelling. SMITH is home of
the Six-Word Memoir® project, now a bestselling book series,
calendar, board game, live event series and global phenomenon.
For more information, visit **www.smithmag.net**.

SMITH Magazine founder Larry Smith has spoken on the
power of storytelling and how to engage a community at
PopTech, SXSW Interactive, AARP'S 50+ convention and
elsewhere. He's spoken and led team-building sessions at
companies such as ESPN, Twitter, Dell, Morgan Stanley,
Google and Shutterfly, as well as at foundations, nonprofits
and schools across the world.

About Reboot

Founded in 2002, Reboot is a nonprofit organization
whose mission is to start discussions about Jewish identity,
community and meaning. Reboot believes that every generation
must grapple with the questions of Jewish identity, community
and meaning on its own terms. Reboot is committed to creating
opportunities for our peers to gather, to engage, to question and
to self-organize in projects such as Sabbath Manifesto,
Sukkah City, the Beyond Bubbie project and more.
For more information, visit **Rebooters.net**.